The King's Donkey
and Other Stories

The King's Donkey
and Other Stories

Written by Mary Richardson
Illustrated by Hilda Joanna

PAULIST PRESS
New York / Mahwah, N.J.

First published in Great Britain in 1976 by
Mayhew McCrimmon Ltd
Great Wakering Essex. © Copyright 1976
and 1985 by Mayhew McCrimmon Ltd.

First published in the United States of
America by Paulist Press copyright
© 1988

ISBN: 0-8091-6574-0

Published by
Paulist Press
997 Macarthur Boulevard
Mahwah, New Jersey 07430

Printed and bound in the U.S.A.

Contents

The King's Donkey

The Children Go to Jesus

Jesus Meets the Fishermen

The King's Donkey

Rebecca was a donkey:
a grey donkey
with long ears.

She belonged to Joel's father,
but it was Joel
who looked after her.
He gave her the finest hay,
and cool spring water,
and brushed her grey coat
every day.
"She is fit to carry a king,"
said Joel's father —

A King as valiant
as David and —

a King as wise
as Solomon.

One day
some men came along.
"You must lend us your donkey,"
they said.
"Why?" Joel's father asked.

"For our King to ride on,"
  they said.
"And who is your King?"
  Joel's father asked.
"It is Jesus of Nazareth,"
  the men said,
  and they untied Rebecca,
  and led her away.

Joel ran after them.
They took off their cloaks
and laid them across
Rebecca's back.
They set Jesus on her
and they rode
slowly forward
to Jerusalem,
the city of King David.

Joel saw men
climbing up the palm trees
and cutting the leaves.
They waved the leaves
and laid them down
in the road
for Jesus to ride over.

Other men took off their cloaks
and spread them out
to make a carpet
for Jesus the King
to ride along.

There were crowds
walking in front of him
and crowds walking behind him
and they were all shouting
"Hosanna!
Blessings on the King!"

Lots of little boys
came running up to Joel
"Come along!" he said.
"It's the son of King David.
Shout hosanna!"
So they all danced along
beside Joel and Rebecca
who was proudly
carrying Jesus.
"Hosanna!
Hosanna!
Hosanna!"
they all shouted.

So everyone called out,
"Peace and glory to God
in the highest heaven!
Blessings on this man
who comes
in the name of the Lord!"
They were very happy
but at last
Jesus got down
from the donkey
and it was all over.
Joel led Rebecca
back home.

What a noise those
boys made!
When they came to the Temple,
the priests said:
"Stop them,"
"No," said Jesus.
"If they kept quiet,
the stones themselves
would cry out."

"That was a wonderful day,"
said Joel.
Rebecca twitched her
long grey ears.
There never had been
and there never would be
another wonderful day
like it in all the world.

The Children
go to Jesus

Ruben and Esther
and little Sarah
lived in a little stone house
at the end of the village.
The lake was in front
and the hill was behind.

There were all sorts of
interesting things to do
when they played together.
Ruben would go fishing
in the lake.

Esther knew where
all the lizards played
at hide-and-seek
among the rocks
on the hillside
and Sarah
who was only three
used to pick handfuls
of gay flowers
to take home.

And once they went
to the sheepfold
on the high hill
and got in the way
of the men
who were driving
the sheep into one pen
and goats into another.
Sarah was afraid of the goats
but Esther gave her
some figs to eat.
They always stopped her crying.

Their friend Nathan lived
in the house next door.
He was a bag of mischief
and when he came to play
with them they did much
more exciting things,
like going to the market
where the fishermen sold
their catch of fishes,

or following the reapers
in the fields
and gathering up the barley
that they dropped —

One fine day Nathan
came running up.
"Quick!
Come to the market place.
Jesus the prophet
from Nazareth is there
and he's talking to everyone
about God his Father
and he's helping people
who are ill.
Come along
and he'll talk to us too."

When they got
to the market place,
they squeezed and squirmed
their way through all the crowd
of men and women,
and they saw Jesus sitting down
talking to people.
He looked wonderfully kind.

But they couldn't get
any nearer to him
because there were
twelve big men
standing round about him.
"Be off,"
they said to Nathan,
and Ruben and Esther
and Sarah.
"Can't you see Jesus is busy?
Away with you!"

Little Sarah began to cry
and forgot to eat her fig.
Nathan, Ruben
and Esther didn't cry,
but they stood still,
very, very disappointed.
They did so want
to talk to Jesus.

Suddenly Jesus looked up.
He saw the children
and the tears in their eyes
and he saw the twelve big men
keeping them away.
"No," he said.
"You must let the children
come to me."

He opened his arms wide
and smiled,
and Nathan, Ruben,
Esther and little Sarah
ran up to him.
The twelve big men
moved aside
and Jesus said to them:
"I like listening to children
You must be like them too,
and enjoy life with me."
The twelve big men
looked at the children
and wondered how —

But the children talked to Jesus
about all the things they did,
and the games they played,
and the way their mothers
and fathers looked after them,
and the good things
they liked eating
and the hard things
they didn't like doing
and the times they squabbled,
and the fun they had with
the lizards and the fishes.
And Jesus laughed and listened
with all his might.

And Sarah sat on Jesus's knee.
She didn't say much
because she was happily
eating her fig.
But she made Jesus
have a bite too,
and he said:
"Thank you Sarah."

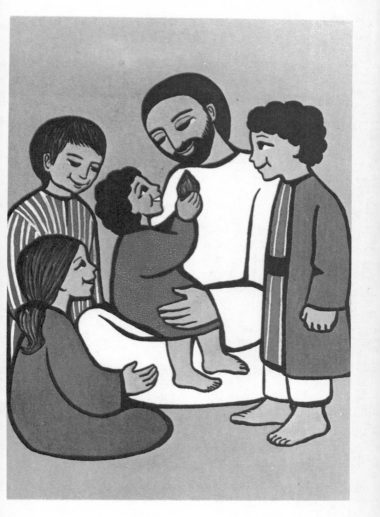

Jesus meets
the Fishermen

There were hundreds
and hundreds of fishes
in the Lake of Galilee
— big fish and little fish,
fish that were tasty
and fish that would
give you a pain inside
if you ate them,
rare fish and common fish
— all swimming round together.

Four fishermen lived by
the Lake of Galilee.
Simon and his brother Andrew
had a boat.
James and his brother John
had a boat
and they all had strong nets
to catch the fish that swam
in the Lake of Galilee.

They used to go out
at night when shoals of fish
were moving round
and then they cast their nets
with a splash and a gurgle
into the water and —

sometimes they caught
dozens and dozens
of fishes and —

sometimes they caught
nothing at all.

In the morning
when the sun
was high in the sky,
they pulled their boats
up to the beach
and sat and mended
their nets.

One day a man came
walking along the beach
with the sun shining
in his face.

He stopped and looked long
at Simon and Andrew
and James and John
on the beach of
the Lake of Galilee.

"Follow me," he said.

At once
Simon and Andrew
dropped their nets.
James and John
clambered out of their boat.
"It's Jesus," they said.

They forgot about their boats
and their nets
and the fishes
in the Lake of Galilee.
They ran up to Jesus.
"Here we are," they said.
"Now I will make you
fishers of men," Jesus said,
and he walked on.

Simon and Andrew
and James and John
followed him.
They were very happy
but they were puzzled
as well.
They were fishers of fish.
Jesus had said,
fishers of men,
I wonder what he meant,
said Peter and Andrew
and James and John,
but —

Next day
they heard Jesus
talking about his Father,
and all sorts of people
came up to him to listen.
There were strong men
and kind women
and happy children,
people who were well
and people who were ill
and miserable,
rich men,
poor men,
beggarmen and thieves,
every sort of person you
could think of,
all gathered together.

It was just what happened
to the fishes
when Simon and Andrew
and James and John
cast their nets into
the Lake of Galilee
So they helped Jesus
to cast his net into
the Lake of the World,
and they caught you.
Glory be to God!